EDEN *miniatures*

EDEN *miniatures*

Dimensions
Heart
The Snowflake Collector
The Ice King
The Planet Walk
The Tape
Istanbul
Sedartis
Encounters
The Bournemouth & Boscombe Trilogy
Insomnia
Euphoria

HEART

Optimist

Heart

First Edition

Heart was first published as part of *EDEN by FREI – a concept narrative in the here & now about the where, the wherefore and forever* at *EDENbyFREI.net*

ISBN: 978-1-64370-451-7

Optimist Books by Optimist Creations

optimistcreations.com

Heart

1 Juice

Of course, I think, for a moment, he didn't actually say that, I just heard that, I just imagined him saying that, I just made that up, because I think it would be interesting. Or would it?

I realise I need to press pause. But he looks at me with this frankness, still, with this openness. If only I could remember meeting me then, then it might make more sense for him to be saying he imagines himself meeting me now. Or was it a joke? I don't remember being much given to jokes. I don't think I was humourless, though I was, undoubtedly, earnest.

I need to press pause, metaphorically, on these 'proceedings' (they're not really going anywhere fast) and allow myself to remember what mattered. And what didn't. Before I say anything more. But can I leave him just hanging there, right in front of me? I can't. Can I just ignore what he's said as if he hadn't said it and I had just imagined him saying it? I could, but that might be rude, and rudeness is unacceptable, therefore I can't. Can I ask him if he really meant that, if he actually knows who I am? Well, I can, but say he doesn't know who I am, say it was just a throwaway remark, say it was just me being a little bit clever, a tiny tad 'interesting', at the age of twenty, twenty-one, then how do I explain to him what I mean, without disturbing his own reality? Is his reality not already disturbed? Mine certainly is. But then I also realise I'm suddenly rather enjoying this.

Up until almost this precise moment I had been greatly disconcerted—not in a profoundly distressed or let alone panicked manner, just really, really unsure of what on earth was going on—but now, maybe jolted by his answer, I feel I've just come up for air. I can float in this sea of uncertainty now. Accept it for what it is, even not knowing what it is. That, it strikes me as suddenly obvious, will have to somehow become my new state of being, for quite some time.

I give him a smile that says, 'I do understand,' although clearly I don't, and enquire just a nudge further: 'I mean in life, what do you see yourself doing?'

His skin is incredibly smooth. I don't recall touching my skin when it was that smooth, that soft. I don't feel like touching it now, though I do wish I could hold him, just to make him feel safe. Then again, I rarely if ever did not feel safe at that age, and seeing that this is me not some stranger—although for all I know about or of him, he might as well be an alien—I just look at him, look at me. 'You're a writer,' I say, not questioning, stating.

'I am,' he says, happy, it seems, that this is so evident; though: 'how did you guess?'

Ah. That turns everything around once more. He doesn't know who I am. How could he, in his life I don't yet exist, other than perhaps in his imagination, but then I remember that at his age I was certain—not vaguely inclined to believe, but convinced—that I would never make it to forty, and here I am, pushing fifty.

I had said so, to my best friend, Peggy: she was appalled. 'How can you say a thing like that?' she'd exclaimed upon my assertion, aged nineteen or twenty, that I would not make it to forty. But I saw no reason to be scandalised: for me, when I was aged nineteen or twenty, the idea alone of ever being as ancient as forty was simply absurd. Surely everything—but *everything!*—worthwhile experiencing, doing, saying or, for that matter, writing, would have been experienced, done, said and most certainly written by then.

I have already outlived my target then by some ten years, and I know now of course that he can't know who I am because not only doesn't he know yet that I exist, he doesn't even believe that I will ever exist. Not because he's being obstreperous or deliberately controversial or simply obtuse, but because he genuinely can't imagine it.

This is my chance, this is my opportunity for a pause: if I can make him think then I'll get the time to think too. There must be, there *must* be a link between him and me.

'I saw your notepad and pen,' I say, playing the 'I'm an observer kind of a person' card.

He now for the second time does something that moves me: he shows me the pad. I take that, before I can think it through, as a signal of trust. And I read. As I read, I remember well having written those words. I have my pause button. I have a clasp on my heart. I have left the dimensions I was travelling through to get here. I can, at last, reconcile.

Or at least I can try...

i should point out
that i'm not real

the
juice
that courses through my body
is not
squeezed
by ordinary means

i want to know how things happen.
i want to know how it happens that you see
somebody
not even meet them
see somebody
from a distance
enter a room, for example
and think
(you don't
think, you go, though
just to yourself:)
'yes

that's him
that's
the one'
(even though you know
it will turn out
that it isn't)

how does this happen
it's ludicrous
you don't even know him:
it is
insane

i
undress him in my mind, imagine him
naked.
i don't do this immediately
it's not something i
jump to
like a conclusion
it's something i resist for a moment
then for another

and for another
until enough moments have passed
an hour or so later, maybe two (sometimes
a whole day or more may pass before i feel it
is
acceptable
before i feel ready) to imagine him
naked. i
touch
his body in my mind, his
chest, my
extended fingers spread, gently run
over the mound of his biceps:
delectable
my
other hand now cups around his waist, just
above his
hip
and draws him a little closer, close enough
that i can
when i lower my head
just a little

inhale
the scent of his
body
musk with a warm sweet sweat of
excitement

i
zonk out of it
just in time: i don't want him
there yet
not yet, we have not even yet said

hello

2 Memories of the Present: Hangover

There is a connection; the connection may well be the pattern. I did this back then, I do this right now; I will be doing this in two years' time, most likely in ten, maybe even in twenty. I understand it, I can put reason to it, but I can't make any sense of it, because reason doesn't really come into it.

I have to sometimes save myself from myself, but more often than not the universe protects me from what I want. If the universe and my subconscious were in tune with each other, then that would explain a lot, even if my conscious still struggles. And it still struggles. I think. And I think sometimes I am my own worst enemy, because I think matters through; I most likely overthink them.

My sitting here now may well be a case in point: I should probably just get drunk with myself on cocktails and not care one jot why I am here now reminding myself of my incapacity to fruitfully fall in love. Even the idea of fruitfully falling in love sounds like a great misunderstanding. Of myself, by myself. Of other people. Namely the people I somehow find myself falling 'in love' with. I wouldn't know the first thing about what that would actually entail. But I know more or less what it wouldn't.

I'm reminded of something that is happening simultaneously, even as I'm talking to George, right now; although of course it isn't, it will have happened either just before or just after, or a little earlier or a little later, but at this moment it might as well be happening right now for the presence it has, the way it imposes itself: I wake up surrounded by paint pots – pots of paint small and large, some tin, some plastic, plus white spirit.

My head aches like Alaska; I open my eyes and close them again and open them once more and then close them again. I hear the voice of my friend Maxl who is staying with me talk to his girlfriend on Skype. His side of the conversation goes, 'uhm... yah... – ... – ...yoah... – ... – ...hmmmyoh.' He's German, more specifically, Bavarian. He may be the first Bavarian I have ever fancied. I used to go much more for lean, lanky tall men, and while I still have a residual primal propensity towards tall people quite generally, I was here for the first time smitten with somebody of a more stoically solid build.

I listen with my eyes closed, though I try not to hear. I used to think that his girlfriend was the most boring person alive, but that may well have been just the tint of jealousy. I don't like the idea of being jealous any more than I like the idea of being angry or ungenerous, but since he's been staying with me, I've realised that my friend—whom I used to have a very soft spot for and whom I continue to hold in a great deal of affection and high professional admiration—when he feels like it (my in this moment murky mind wants to say: when he's under her spell), can be almost as boring as she, even though his name doesn't suggest it; his name suggests mischief and a boyish irreverence and a sense of adventure and a laugh and a roll in the hey and an ice cream too many and a drink on top, and calling on Freddie at two in the morning quite tipsy, and an eagerness to discover. None of which is currently much on display, but we did once call on Freddie at two in the morning after a party, as Freddie happened to live on the way home, in Berlin. That was fun. (The girlfriend wasn't amused...)

Maxl. He sleeps a hell of a lot. Maybe he's depressed. Or maybe his girlfriend tires him out. She is very hard work, I realise. He sleeps more than I think he's awake, and sometimes he's asleep when awake, and even when he's awake he often might as well be asleep. He's been here for five months now and he still doesn't speak English. That puzzles me. I must be hungry and hungover. Hence, surely, my state of mind which, to my own baffled unease, seems to signal malfunction: I've never known myself so discomfited by a person I love.

My brain hurts.

One of the paint pots has leaked pinkish paint onto my pillow, it looks oddly svelte. There is no better cure for an infatuation with someone than to have them stay at your flat for a while. I used to think he was the one, and I came close to telling him so. I certainly told him his girlfriend was boring. I don't regret that, it was true. Right now I wish myself buried under twelve thousand pebbles. Not dead, just buried. The pebbles would soothe me and ward off the 'yahem... – ... – och – ... – nyah' litany of... *what* exactly? I keep my eyes closed and try to drift off. It's not easy...

{Petals}

I think I can count on one hand (plus maybe one finger, perhaps even two, three at a stretch) the number of people I have actually fallen in love with. This surprises me, because I think not all the hairs I now have on my head and in my beard combined would suffice to account for the number of people I think I have fallen in love with. There is, as always, a margin of error, but it is nowhere near as wide as one might imagine:

Benjamin (First and Most Deeply). Stefan (Under Special Circumstances). Janey (Somewhat Unexpectedly). The Man Whose Name I Can't Remember Who Stage Managed One of the Tours I Was on (Though I'm Not Sure How That Even Happened Because The Moment I Fell

Out of Love With Him I Wondered What Did I Ever See in Him and Wrote a Song to That Effect). The Willow (Of Course, and Still Am a Little, and He Knows it). Probably JayJay (In a Singular Way). Certainly Dominic. A Little Bit Edward. And Indeed Moritz. Actually that brings me up to nine. But already I'd need to qualify. Was I really *in love* with Stefan? Or was I just blown away by how beautiful, charming and unimaginably cute he was?

There are many, many more I have at some point been a little in love with and still am, somewhere on the scale where it nearly registers, sometimes a bit more, then back to a bit less. And there are many, many whom I simply love. Roundly, completely, for who they are. And there are borderline cases. Michael, at school. Was I actually 'in love' with him, or did I 'just' love him, as I most certainly did. And before him the

English boy who came to our school in Switzerland on some exchange programme.

He was almost certainly the first person I ever had a genuine crush on. I was maybe eleven or twelve and he'd arrived into one year below or above, I believe, and I was so smitten that I bought him an ice cream. That was all: on our way to school there was a kiosk where everybody bought their sweets, and although he wasn't in my year and we hadn't been introduced and I didn't know his name, I just felt compelled to let him know that I liked him, and so I bought him an ice cream. I gave it to him and he smiled and said thank you, and I don't remember ever saying another word to him, but to this day it makes me happy to think of the moment he smiled at me, a little surprised, but friendly, and gracious in a way I had never seen anybody smile before and have rarely seen anyone smile since: that brief and simple but in retrospect devastating moment when innocence meets recognition.

I realise this is something I should ask myself. Something that maybe could help me today. I could learn maybe something from George. That makes sense. Much more, in fact, than the idea that he could learn anything from me. I could perhaps learn from him how he did that. How he set up a pattern that to this day I haven't escaped; he's much closer to it, he's in the process of doing it now: what is going on in his head; what, more to the point, in his heart? Obviously I can't phrase my question like that, I obviously have to go about it smidgeonwise more dextrously.

But if I played this one right, I might actually gain some insight...

3 Chaos

This makes me wonder what, in a multiverse of all possible universes, my life is like right now in the world where Benjamin and I are together.

So often have I tried to find him in others—repeatedly have I attempted to find him himself—that I've lost all concept of what the reality would be of us actually having done what other people do. Do other people do this? It's certainly the impression I get: other people I know meet someone, fall in love, have some ups and downs, decide to give it a go, give it a go, stick together, or sometimes not, and if they don't then most likely they have a break and then either give it another go, or do so with somebody else. I have good examples at close range of things working out well between people, all around me. My family, especially, are exemplary. So it shouldn't be difficult. Still, it mystifies me.

Benjamin has fallen out with his father, this much I know. I know this much because the last number I find in my old address book for him is his old home number, and at one point, while I'm in the country, I phone that number and I get his dad on the phone who tells me that he doesn't know where his son is. Nor how to contact him. He says this quite categorically, and I'm surprised, of course, and a bit stunned, and about to end the conversation, but before I do I ask whether anybody else might know how to contact him, and he says, yes, his mother might know. Ah, I say, and would he happen to still have a number for his mother. I sense I need to tread carefully as I don't want to upset or offend him, and I feel sorry that they're no longer together, but at least that offers a plausible explanation as to why his father does not know where he is or how to contact him: his parents must have separated many years ago, maybe on bad terms. But: 'this number here,' he says; 'she'll be back later, she's at work now.'

This now saddens more than it puzzles me, and it puzzles me a lot: clearly Benjamin's mother and father are still together, still living in the same house where I once or twice came to see him, where I met both of them, once or twice; where in fact I interviewed his dad for my final school project, which I wrote on racism; but while his mother 'may know' how to get in touch with him, the father not only doesn't know, he obviously doesn't want to know either. His son is dead to him. A wave of abject sadness washes over me. He is, has always been, so alive to me.

Should it surprise that your first love is your strongest, your most intensely felt, most devastating and also most exulted? To this day I remember getting drunk on coffee with him on the sofa. That seems surreal now, but we drank so much coffee over so many hours all through the night until it was getting light outside, I started feeling high. Caffeine and adrenaline and serotonin. And that other thing. Is there that other thing, that indescribable thing, that thing we sing songs about and write poems over and feel we could die for?

I phoned up again a day or two later (or maybe it was later that day) and spoke to the mother who remembered me and may have remembered me fondly, she certainly sounded warm and kind, and she said, yes, if I were to write him a letter she would forward it onto him, that might work.

I wrote him a letter, and she forwarded it onto him and nothing happened for a very long time; and I remembered—as I spoke to his mother and before I wrote the letter—the birthday for which I had sent him a flower. He lived outside Zürich then, I outside Basel; his birthday was and still is six days before mine, and because I couldn't see him on his birthday, I went out and bought him a flower—I can't be sure now what kind of flower it was, but I like to think and am fairly certain it was a yellow rose—and I asked the florist for one of those small vials that would keep the flower fresh for a while, and I sealed this around the stem of the flower and wrapped it in tissues in case it should leak and sealed that in foil, I believe, and then put the flower into a long box, and I must have used some padding, and then I posted it to him, with my birthday wishes. I didn't wonder then but I wondered now what his mother made of this at the time.

I wrote him a letter and sent it to his mother, and she forwarded it to him and nothing happened for a very long time until one Sunday the phone rang and it was Benjamin. Out of the blue, except for the letter of course. He'd received it, and now he was living in Guggisberg. He'd moved to Guggisberg because of the song, did I know it? I didn't, but I know it now.

We talked for maybe four or five hours. I don't remember what we talked about, but then it was that kind of connection that we'd always had: where you can talk for four or five hours and not remember what you talked about, nor really care. For those four or five hours it was as if he were there.

And all of a sudden I can feel it ease, the pain of not knowing what had become of Benjamin. He's not had an easy ride. 'I have a son,' he says. 'I have a tooth missing.' He's been through addiction and rehab and back, and other things. He lives with his partner, who isn't the mother of his son.

'You've done a good thing here,' he said, meaning my writing to him, and after the afternoon had passed with us talking, he said, 'and now I'm going to get drunk.' We were a bit drunk already, again, both of us, this time on the beers we each started to open, he in Guggisberg, I in Earl's Court.

'And I'm going to hear Jane Birkin in concert,' I said, and it was true. He wasn't online, but he would write back to me now, he said; but I didn't think he would, and he didn't.

After a few months or so, maybe a year, I thought I'd just write to him one more time, although I was myself no longer sure of the wisdom of doing so, and I sent another letter, this time directly to him, at the address he'd given me, on the Guggisberg. It came back as not delivered: the addressee has moved away. But now I don't mind. My heart is light and free. I hope before either of us dies I'll see him again, maybe when we're quite old. Maybe when we're quite old we can sit together on a bench or in a lakeside cafe and spend a whole day talking, maybe getting drunk a little. On whatever.

I look at George looking at me, and I remember I'm not alone. I've never been alone, I've always had George, but George has been very much on his own at times; he has chosen a lone path, and I can't blame him for that. 'Tell me about

Benjamin,' I want to say, but I now know everything I need to know about him, and I know that George knows much less now than I.

I walk into a room full of people. It's the Christmas Bazar at the Steiner School in Zürich. I've gone there with a friend from Basel, to visit a couple of people we'd met at a Whitsun Camp earlier in the year and stayed in touch with. I don't remember anything else about the day, not how we arranged to meet, or who else was there. Most likely we'd just arrived, and most likely we'd said: in the cafe, around then. The cafe is just a class room, converted for the day; or maybe it's a small hall. I remember the feel of a converted class room. The room is full, there is a table with five or six people at it, in conversation. Two or three of them we already know. To the others, we introduce ourselves. One of them turns around: *'Ich bi dr Benjamin.'* My world has never been the same again.

'Tell me, George,' I finally say, the Mojito giving me licence to talk: 'what do you make of the heart?'

4 Maxl (Still Here)

I wake up to a horrible dream. It's so horrible I don't want to think about it, it could well be the second most horrible dream I've ever had, and I take issue with horribleness, so I go back to sleep once again and I don't continue to dream, which I'm glad on.

Maxl knocks on the door and wakes me up; I'm already half awake but that means I'm also half asleep and I'm hugging a pillow for comfort. He asks if I'm all right; I am puzzled: he's never been this concerned about me before. He says he's concerned about me.

Maybe I made horrible noises in my horrible dream, it's possible. I blink at him and say, 'yes,' and I'm about to go back to sleep once again; he says, 'it's nearly half two,' which in German means half one but means nothing to me at the moment because they've put the clocks forward last night and I don't do mornings well at the best of times.

Maxl rustles about in my room while I drift back off to sleep. He keeps much of his stuff in my room, so it's a bit like having a live-in partner, without the partner, it's a bit like a lose-lose situation: the worst of both worlds. The good thing I suppose: we don't argue. Though he moans at me.

Maxl moans at me about England. For England: every day he comes back from college or from the bank or from the tube or from the post office or from the supermarket or from the park or from the cafe or from the pub or from the pavement, moaning at me. Every day.

He is German so he's used to hyper-efficiency; he also lives in Berlin when he's not here, so he's used to an agreeable level of anarchic socialism. Objectively, I agree with most of what he complains about, but the complaining itself bugs me, every day, about everything.

That and the fact that he moans at me in German: he makes it sound as if I were responsible. Maybe I am responsible. Maybe my quiet acquiescence to all things British, to all things English, to all things London, has made me complicit in bringing about a college that charges an arm and a leg but that has embarrassingly poor facilities and a bunch of students who, instead of standing up for their ideas and their rights and their freedoms, do everything they're told, as they're told, and for a bank that charges an arm and a leg in fees and makes opening a bank account as much of a deal as if you were asking the Emperor of China for a slice of Tibet, and a tube that charges you an arm and a leg but shuts down for weekends at a time and that runs late because one of their drivers has a bout of the sniffles and that goes on strike at the whiff of a comma being changed in a staff manual and that stops running at midnight when half the population is still about town enjoying themselves, and for a post office that I can't think of what they might be doing wrong off the top of my head but I can easily imagine that in Germany they run their post offices in a way that is altogether more, well, German, and for a supermarket that installs machines that talk at you instead of employing people who serve you, and for a park that is actually pretty much perfect if you ask me but that if you're German you'll probably nevertheless find something to moan about, and for the cafe that I can't I'm losing my will to live...

The pubs close too early, I know, and the trains are a nightmare, get over it, it's London, this, innit.

I can't be doing with this much moaning and I realise that much as I love him, if Maxl were my husband I would have to ask him for a divorce right now. That would be terrible. Fortunately he's only a very good friend and I can love him even though he moans at me because I know I don't have to own any of this beyond the level to which I just have to own my share of this culture that so irks him. Better still, much as I love Berlin—and I love Berlin, and I always, always still keep a metaphorical suitcase there—I don't have to move to Berlin with him just because he doesn't like London. I actually think he quite likes London, which also makes me think that maybe moaning is just a default state of his, and so he maybe also moans about Berlin! At his girlfriend! *(Phew!)*

I don't know, and I don't want to speculate because I'm troubled by my horrible dream, which I don't want to think about, and I also don't want to seem ungrateful or ungracious or ungenerous. I don't want to seem or to feel un-anything. I love Maxl (I've changed his name here, by the way, because I don't want to get him into trouble, nor do I want him to think that I don't love him just because he moaned at me), and I am grateful to him for being a good, loyal friend, and I graciously accept the gift of insight that even someone you love can get on your nerves to the point where you are quite prepared to wrestle them to the ground and slap them with a very wet fish, and I want to retain and hold on to the generosity of spirit that says, live and let live, love and let love, be and let be. And I realise I am actually moaning about somebody moaning at me. Which is a little ironic. And I like little ironies. Though I still don't like moaning. Which I suppose makes it doubly ironic... And the whole experience reminds me *acutely* why I so much enjoy being single.

I feel tempted to tell George about this, but obviously I don't because I don't want to prejudice him against Maxl or against me. And I certainly don't want to tell him about the horrible dream, which he'd be bound to want to hear more about, the way I know George...

{Contentment}

If everything were perfect, as it is, how much would we crave disturbance?

The variants that made matter congeal. The idiom that expresses just what needs to be said. The waves within waveforms that ripple through time.

There are connections that never make sense, but they make me feel that I am a part of something. No-one knows what. The friend of my nephew who is so gentle, so unassuming and yet so lovely. His exquisite taste. His mild and agreeable manner. His beautiful face. His warm and unfussy friendship. His ease that isn't untroubled but that knows how to hold on to the core. His generous smile. His diligent gestures as he cooks us a meal that tastes like a dish for the gods. The faintly-haired legs that end in two so shapely feet. I could be here. This presence is one I could glow in forever. I'm sure.

Will ever I be able to find this and know that I have found it?

5 Surrender

There are plenty of reasons to suppose that we should, and should be able to, learn. In every other sphere of life this seems to work just fine: you burn your hand on the hot handle of a saucepan on the hob, you know better next time. Maybe not next time, but the time after. You wobble on your bike a few yards as a boy with your older brother or your friends or your dad holding on to it and they shout 'go!' and 'faster!' and you go faster and they let go of the bike and you stay upright and you have the hang of it and you can now ride a bike. You may still fall off occasionally, but the principle is down and you can tick that off your list. You practise and practise and practise the piano and if you have a modicum of talent and a bit of a musicality in your ear you will become passably good at playing. If you have a lot of talent and a great deal of musicality and an abundant love for what you are doing you may become exceptionally good and turn into a professional musician, a concert pianist; if you are god's gift to improvisational jazz, you may become Keith Jarrett. Languages. Mathematics. History. Even writing, people even teach writing, which suggests people learn it. Chemistry. Not love though. Not the chemistry of love. Not the mystery of love. Not the vexation of love. Not the love of love.

Lukas (who's not really called Lukas either, I'm changing his name too, though I doubt he will read this, and if he does, I doubt he will recognise himself, and if he did, I doubt he would mind) does to me what dozens of men before him have done, never deliberately, hardly ever even aware, most certainly not with any ill intentions: he infatuates me. In him. Is infatuate a transitive verb? In a passive sense? If I am now infatuated, that would suggest I have been infatuated and since I can hardly infatuate myself—unless I sport a substantial streak in narcissism—the person who infatuates should, if logic had anything to do with it, by definition be the infatuator, with the person who's infatuated the infatuatee. Logic has very little to with it.

Lukas is a little taller than me and a little younger. I've always wanted to be a little taller than I am (though I am not, by averages, short), and while I spent the whole of my teens wanting to be older, and never really in that sense since have wanted to be substantially younger than I actually am, I relate well to people who are a little younger, partly because part of my brain has not really caught up yet with my actual age, and partly because another part of my brain has always been far ahead. Age doesn't really matter to me. Or so I like to believe, though the seconds ticking away so implacably, two and a half billion of them, give or take a few: that troubles me.

Lukas (and I like the name Lukas, not least because I now associate it with the man I have off the top of my head given it to), is German, though you wouldn't immediately think so: his accent makes him sound more like a Dutchman who's spent a lot of time in the States, or a Europeanised American. He and his girlfriend have joined the choir together, and on the first evening of the new term he sits next to me, and I feel like a schoolboy. I feel like the schoolboy precisely who fell in love with Michael when he joined our class, he aged seven, most of us then aged eight. This is ridiculous. I know it is ridiculous, and my young brain infuriates at the idiocy of my heart, while my old brain manages a smile that sits halfway between condescending and indulgent. Of course you are now infatuated, it says, my old brain, to heart. Worry not. Like all previous infatuations this one shall pass, and you will laugh about it later. Soon, in fact, because I have so much experience now, so much insight—very nearly wisdom—to give you and to ease the imminent transition from infatuation to friendship imbued with love of the friendship kind, a love that is unentangled, appreciative, mutual, but free.

You idiot! says my younger brain, you child, you pubescent teenager: you, at the age of fifty are allowing yourself a crush on somebody who has just introduced you to his girlfriend and who is absolutely certain to fancy you about as much as his grandfather's drinking pal Ralph. (I like the idea of Lukas having a grandfather with a drinking pal called Ralph, and I feel slightly flattered that I should remind him of him. That's how absurd I am at this moment...) There is nothing to be done. When he misses a couple of rehearsals, I miss him. When he returns, my heart leaps. In the break, when he's standing, chatting to his girlfriend, I join them. I make a point of talking to her as much as to him, so she doesn't feel left out, but I really only have eyes for him. It is totally ridiculous, even pathetic, but thoroughly enjoyable too.

Maybe that's what this is about: maybe the reason the heart won't learn is not just because it doesn't really have to, and not so much because it can't, but simply because it doesn't actually want to: the pleasure of being a little in love, of being infatuated, of being just a tad drugged by endorphins is just too great to forego forever. And why should it: this kind of love doesn't cause any harm. It's not even causing pain, curiously. In the past it did. In the past, I would get over my infatuations through pain. That is no longer the case. Probably because while the heart steadfastly refuses to learn, the head is really quite capable now of putting it all in its place.

Also in the choir is another sweet man who is quite a bit younger and quite a bit shorter and maybe also a little bit rounder than me. And he's roundly adorable too. I just want to hug him, every time I see him. He reminds me of Paddington Bear. How could you not cuddle Paddington Bear? And until not so long ago there was a young man who was just very beautiful. Or so I thought. I don't think I ever spoke more than about three and half sentences with him. And of course there was Edward...

George looks at me puzzled. 'I think you should go with the heart,' he finally says in a calm measured tone, looking me straight in the eye. I'm momentarily stumped until—dragged out of my reverie—I remember my question: what does he make of the heart?

'Really?' I surprise myself with my surprise. I mean: I agree with him, but isn't he the one who too often has precisely not done that, and now he's telling me?... 'Yes.' He speaks with a slight accent and a tone that makes him sound a little aloof and a little bemused and a little detached and a little curious, too. I remember being all of these very well, but I don't remember sounding them. 'The only times I've ever been unhappy was when I did not follow my heart. You know: "you regret the things you haven't done, never the things you did..."' Yes, but: you're telling *me?* If I

knew this then, and he's probably right, I knew this then, then how come I still make exactly the same mistakes?... hang on. Did I not just say they're not, maybe, mistakes, at all, they're maybe just: my *modus operandi.*

'Assuming, George, you could find the ideal partner for yourself, who would that be?'

'Oh I don't think such a person exists.' – He doesn't even have to think about it.

'Why do you think so?' I'm beginning to feel a little inadequate, talking to myself, aged twenty-one.

'Well, because there is no ideal person. For anyone. People just accommodate each other and get used to each other's foibles, and when they find somebody who they can bear more than they can bear being alone, they settle with them; for as long as that's true, and sometimes quite a bit longer, mainly because they can't be bothered going through the hassle of separation. Or because they're comfortable enough. Or because they're afraid.'

'And you?'

'Oh I'm not afraid.'

I thought as much, but:

'Can you bear being alone?'

'I love being on my own. I love being with people, and I love being on my own. I need a lot of time and a lot of space for myself. I function exceptionally well on my own.'

That is so true. That was true then, that is true now. Thank you, George: I function exceptionally well, on my own. Thank you. But does that necessarily mean I couldn't function even better with someone? Ah, here we go again...

6 Domesticity

Why would anyone not put their milk in
the fridge? Is this a male thing: do men, as
a rule, not put their milk back in the fridge,
whence clearly it came from? It bothers me.

Maxl drinks green milk, semi-skimmed.
I don't see the point of anything semi,
let alone semi-skimmed; the green cap
is not for me. I abhor the idea of milk
that is skimmed of its fat of its taste of its
goodness of its milky nature, as I abhor
decaffeinated coffee, artificial sweetener
and non-alcoholic beer. They are, as far as
I'm concerned, abominations. They are,
if not abominations, man-made oxymora.
They are the kind of contradiction in terms
that I, at the risk of sounding judgmental,
find wholly unnecessary. And necessarily
unholy...

Maxl pours over his muesli green milk; it actually looks green, the colour is all wrong. It looks wrong it feels wrong it sounds wrong. The word 'semi' sounds wrong, as does the word 'skimmed'.

Maxl pours green milk over his muesli and then leaves the milk out of the fridge for the rest of the day. Although it bothers me, I don't strictly mind, as it's his milk, and being green it probably won't go off, as it's basically watery cow juice that has had all the goodness skimmed off it. This milk is no cheese in the making. Also, I'm hardly someone who uses his kitchen in a sanctified manner. I am no chef. Things lying or standing about my kitchen are generally not in my way.

I don't mind, but it bothers me, and I wonder what makes a man leave his milk out of the fridge: is it an innate desire, a need to mark your territory with some whitish liquid, signalling your existence? I've never known a woman to leave out her milk; women know how precious milk is, they don't care for milk that turns yellow and rancid. Men don't mind yellow and rancid, it's part of their being.

Maxl leaves his milk out and sometimes, too, his salami. I read nothing into this, I just note it and wonder: what is it that makes men leave their milk out, and, occasionally, their salami. That is all. That, and the fact that it bothers me. That fact bothers me in turn, as I like to think of myself as the kind of person who would not be bothered by anything near so trivial.

Does it mess with my sense of territory after all? Or with my sense of order? Or my sense of propriety? It may be the fact alone that it's green milk, not real milk, that he leaves out of my fridge: I probably deep down feel that my kitchen is being sullied by the presence of fake, pretend milk. Perhaps, even though rationally I know it has absolutely no meaning, it deep down offends me. The way it offends me, deep down, when I find in my fridge bottles of Coca-Cola left by house guests, although they invariably turn out to be useful, as Coke is excellent for clearing the drain.

I resolve to leave things be as they are and not trouble too much about matters so insignificant such as these. At least, I think, I don't have to put up with this kind of behaviour for any length of time, and I certainly don't have to own it: we are not in a relationship, we are not cohabiters, we are not even flatmates: he is a guest, and the law of hospitality stipulates that he can do with his milk—the top of which may be any colour of his choosing—whatever he likes, for as long as he likes, just as long as he doesn't expect me to endorse or approve it. Which clearly he doesn't: he's completely oblivious to absolutely any of this, and he doesn't even notice if I put his milk back where I think—inadequate and green though it be—it belongs: in the fridge.

7 The Space Boy

He is a quietly spoken wonder, a boy
who has never grown up; a spacealien of
the loveliest nature, a Zebedee who has
bounced off his Magic Roundabout and
somehow found himself in a world full of
people: I adore him.

Where Laniakea's fibrous filaments' ends
disentangle from her neighbour's, to float,
as jellyfish through water, amid dark matter
in slow, rhythmic pulses, the Space Boy
has sought out a moment of respite for
comfort and warmth and sat down with me
in a Camden pub with a pint each of ale,
autumn time.

I love him, Space Boy, in a way I love few.
He's about to get married. He doesn't mean
to marry; every signal his subconscious

mind emits says he doesn't want to, and every action that his conscious mind commands says he must.

He doesn't send out his invitations, he forgets arrangements, postpones, prevaricates. He talks, on the verge of getting drunk with me, about the revelation his sister-in-law-to-be gave him when she told him it was a continuum, not an either thing or an or, a this thing or that. Clearly he senses himself on that spectrum, somewhere towards the brighter colours, but, that light notwithstanding, he's lost. Will no-one hie to his rescue?

I can't. I once nearly did. We'd stood facing each other, our hands on each other's arms; and our lips almost touched. Then his brother walked in and the moment had gone: the night was spent in separate corners of the universe; I in mine, he in his. With that moment gone, all moments like it were gone, but my affection for him hasn't waxed or waned like the moon, nor shall it: steady as a star it remains, even now that he doesn't want to and knows he doesn't want to but knows he is about to tie himself in a knot.

Laniakea drawing away from Perseus-Pisces. I have a feeling this isn't slow. The more I look at the Space Boy and listen to him expound on the vibrations, on the music of the spheres, on how tuned we are into each other, the more I know that what to us seems imperceptibly slow and unfathomably deep and incomprehensibly vast and impenetrably dark is bursting with energy, is replete with substance, is contained in a thought, and is teeming, teeming with life; and with life comes death and with death comes disintegration and with disintegration comes decomposition and with decomposition come component particles and with component particles come clusters of mass that attract each other and with clusters of mass that attract each other come new constellations and with new constellations come configurations and with configurations come potentialities and with potentialities come energy fields and with energy fields comes communication and with communication comes connection and with connection comes communion and communion is love and love is energy and the Space Boy and I are that energy and our minds are a dance and dancing is joy and joy is the present and the present is now and now is forever and forever is what we want it to be...

The Space Boy and I are lying on our backs on the ground looking up at the sky. The sky is plastered with empty silvery foil sleeves into which he will pour his spirited being. 'I never want to not hold you dear,' I whisper and rest my head on his chest looking down into the endlessness that ends where another begins. We are at a synapse in god's brain and god is our own idea of our meaning: no wonder we sense god's grace when we feel the pulse of a heart and bathe in the brainwaves of our fellows, our friends.

The Space Boy leaves me to think myself humble and rich. Has he not travelled light years to be here, to share one thought with me only? I treasure this thought and keep it inside my head where I know it won't be contained: once thought, a thought is already encompassed in our common conscious, and he knows and I know and they know and you; we all know:

We all are one.

8 JoJo

Today is unusual in that it passes slowly. This is unheard of, more or less. For the third time in a row I look at the clock or the watch or the phone and I think, 'ah, it's not gone eleven; oh, it's only just coming up one; hn, it's not even three.' Normally it's, 'what? six o'clock in the afternoon already, I need to get in the shower otherwise I'll be late for the theatre the cinema the drinks or the dinner, or sometimes the gig.'

But today I'm running early and that's unusual and I'm wholly unrushed and wholly unpressured and really quite happy; the sun is out, it's as hot as summer though it's only April, and the time is barely two thirty in the afternoon. All of which is new.

The reason today passes more slowly than usual is probably because I've been up and functional since about ten, and the reason I've been up and functional since about ten is that I woke up about eight, and the reason I woke up about eight is that I went to bed about one, which for me is early, and the reason I went to bed about one is that in bed also was JoJo and I wanted to be with him, and that's unusual too. (I'm changing his name here as well, by the way. Not that not doing so would land him in trouble, or me, for that matter, I don't think, but I don't know whether he'd want to be named and I don't want to ask him because that would seem like making a big deal of things, and I'm not of a disposition to make a big deal of things generally, really.)

Everything's a little different since JoJo's arrived, three days ago. By coincidence, he arrived on the day Maxl departed, and within hours everything changed. Gone is the stuff and the friendly but heavy presence of a man who doesn't really want to be here but doesn't not want to be here either, who seems to lack all sense of humour but still retains a modest charm, who has brilliance concealed by sluggish thinking and earthy inaction.

Gone is the farmer who somehow found himself in a city, who almost by fluke made it to London and into my life where for a while I thought he ought to stay, but from where to know him departed I thank my angels, god, the universe and all that is in and around it, because after I previously had asked all of them for him, they have shown themselves wise and forgiving, by putting him there for me just long enough to see what that would be like, and then, without fuss or damage, taking him away again, no questions asked. Thank you angels, thank you god; universe and all that is in and around you: thank you.

JoJo is more than a breath of fresh air, he's a tonic, a breeze to keep you alive and awake; and he's done what I couldn't expect he would do but still knew he would, he's come back, if only for a few days, and so while we're not sleeping together as in 'sleeping together' now, we're sleeping together as in sleeping together, and I like him next to me in my bed, and sometimes it happens that I snuggle up to him, and when he gets up at an unfeasible hour in the morning to go to work, I briefly stir, sensing him unclasp himself from my probably too firm embrace, and because the sun is already shining and I had a good dinner with him the night before, which he cooked, and because he's the only person I've ever known to come and go like a cat, unperturbed, unencumbered, loyal but free, dictated by his external needs maybe more than by his internal wants but nonetheless appreciative of the shelter, attention and strokes for his warm body and reciprocal appreciation of his comforting presence I can offer, he wandered back into my existence, and I have no idea how long he's going to be here for, but while he's here I am happy, and because I am happy I like to be near him, and so when he's home I go to bed early so I can go to bed with him, and because I go to bed early I wake up calm and rested even though I don't sleep anywhere near as soundly as I do on my own; and the day passes more slowly than it normally does, and I think maybe the day passes more slowly because without knowing it or being aware of it or consciously acknowledging it, I am waiting for him to come back, and part of me wonders if that has a meaning, and an even more reticent part of me wonders if, should it indeed have a meaning, that meaning is that I am slowly changing, at last, and if that is the case then what, exactly, in turn, does that mean?

{Detour}

The incident with the van was unnecessary.

It never really happened, of course, but that, considering how unnecessary it was, may be just as well. I had found myself on the edge of a village called Checkendon, waiting for someone to pick me up from the Cherry Tree Inn where I had spent part of the night. The other, earlier part, I had spent in a converted barn making up words to no end. These words were then taken by four or five individuals of varying degrees of expertise, importance and relevance to the task in hand, and essentially messed around with, much in the way I don't like. Since it was a job I was being paid to do and that I had no emotional investment in, I kept a half-pained smile on my lips and retained some other words within, unspoken.

By 1:30 in the morning it had been decided, by one person or another who was in some way or other involved with the project, that it was now time to call it a night. So Timmah swung on his motorbike, and I was given a lift by someone else to a B&B somewhere in the countryside, where, having had only three hours sleep the previous night, I immediately went to bed but did not immediately fall asleep.

Instead, I lay awake for a few minutes pondering what my life had come to and wondering whether Timmah felt, as I did, that it would be comforting and reassuring now to hold on to each other, to curl up in one bed instead of the two and to rest in each other's arms for a while. The option existed of knocking on his door and asking him outright, but I was too tired, and also—as so very often before—I felt that doing so might just jeopardise our easy and uncomplicated friendship.

I woke up amazingly refreshed. I am not good in the morning. I do not get up and trill a summery tune. I do not sing in the shower. I don't (at this point in my life) yoga and I don't jog. The only time I get to see dawn is when I'm still up from the night before. But the job in the barn appeared to demand that having left there barely six hours earlier, we return and continue the dance of irrelevance. Timmah and I had a hearty breakfast which—it later turned out—I enjoyed more than he did, and he then swung himself back on his bike, while I waited for the shortish man with the blonde eyelashes to drop by and pick me up in his car, as he'd promised to do the night before.

This took a little longer than I expected because apparently he forgot, and so after breakfast I checked out of the B&B and sat myself at a wooden garden table outside the pub, enjoying the early sunshine and continuing to ponder the stark insignificance of my own existence.

I was just getting to the point where I thought there's only so much pondering you can do without anything actually happening, when a rather large man in a larger still van appeared, not quite out of nowhere, but still unannounced. He drove up to nearly as far as he could across the gravelled parking lot—otherwise empty—and purposely decabbed, opened the back, took from it what looked like a plastic tray of something or other and carried it to what one imagines must be the tradesmen's entrance or the kitchen, his protruding belly leading the way.

What happened next is, of course, pure fantasy, but what do you do when you're in the middle of nowhere, called upon to go back to the outskirts of somewhere to pursue the pointless depletion of your brain at the hands of a bunch of people you have nothing in common or store with (except, most certainly, Timmah) and who drain your soul, talking and thinking and living in terms of things that are 'key', when in front of you is a getaway van. Stuff in the back, probably food to last for a week, or at any rate something that has at least some sort of value, intrinsic or not. Engine running. Cab door open. Driver at least twenty, maybe thirty seconds off guard. Possibly more. He'd never dream of somebody doing what I did next. A few seconds passed. Tic. Toc. Toc. Tic. No sign of him yet. Cab door open. Engine running. I would be caught within minutes. Or would I?...

I peel off the pub bench on which I had perched and pick up my backpack, not very large. I take two paces towards the van, maybe three. No sign of the driver. What is he doing? Probably having a chat with chef. Or with the girl at reception, more likely. Twenty paces, twenty-four. Thirty. I'm not really counting. I step up to the door nearest me, passenger side, on the left. The slide across to the driver's seat will be awkward. I unsling my backpack, when:
'Oi!'

Large man looms even larger as he strides towards me red-faced with rage. For once, my brain cells don't desert me. Cool as a cucumber I reach across the wheel and turn off the engine. Slide back down, re-slinging the backpack, and look at him frankly, as he approaches. 'Oh, I'm so sorry, I thought you might be a while...'

Fucking this bloody that and the usual, but my boldness, I believe, stunned him, into submission. He slammed the back shut, heaved himself into his driver's position and, revving loudly, took off. He could have crushed me. Decked me or punched me. Nothing of the sort. He just made his departure loud.

I felt a little prouder that morning than I had done before. Not for infuriating a simple bloke, but for daring myself. Perhaps, I then thought, that's my lesson today: perhaps I should simply adopt a more adventurous lifestyle and push myself further, a little, now and then, to the edge...

9 Dust

Maxl has left and I go over the flat with the Dyson and some degree of resentment, directed not at Maxl, though clearly over the six months or so that he's been here he never once did the same, and neither did I over the six months or so that he's been here, because let's face it: he's the houseguest, does he expect me to go around and clean up after him? Then again, he's the houseguest, so do I expect him to go round and clean up after me? Clearly not. And since neither of us found it necessary to go round the flat with the Dyson for the six months or so that we've been here together, to clean up after each other or let alone after ourselves, there is now a considerable amount of dust about the place.

I end up cleaning up after him because he leaves with a hug and a, 'so this I suppose is goodbye,' which it is only in as much as he's not staying here any longer, he's moving across town to North London and we'll be seeing each other by the end of the week.

And so, no, my resentment is not of Maxl, whom I love and continue to love even though I'm seriously glad he's moved out now, my resentment is with the dust. Dust in itself to me is objectionable to the point of being offensive. Why make people dusty? Isn't that just adding insult to injury? I pause and reflect: what injury? The dust twirls around in the Dyson and I look at it this way instead: the good thing about leaving a little dust to accumulate in the flat is that when then you go round it with a Dyson you really notice the difference. Both in the flat, which suddenly seems altogether less, erm, dusty, but also in the little Dyson which visibly fills up, and you think most of this is just dead skin cells: I litter my space with this; how many Dysons have I filled since, well, ever?...

I look at George and I notice we haven't said anything for a while now, and that has not felt strange, it has felt comfortable. As comfortable as it should when you are sitting opposite yourself—even your much younger self—and you are actually quite happy to be there: with you, but not you. That was now, and this is then. I opt not to ask him any more questions for at least another such moment, and he looks at me and seems content. The moment is so comfortable that I try to remember it from his perspective, and it feels like I can, though it's much more likely that I can't and that I'm just constructing that memory in my mind even as I reflect on it, like a seven-dimensional puzzle. We're coming to the end of our mojitos and I catch Ahmed's eye.

10 Secrets, No Lies

Everything can be true, to a greater or lesser extent.

Is what I imagine any less real than what I say before I do it, and when I do it is it then real or could I forget it and make it undone, or could I apologise for my faults, of which there are many, to myself, even, and having done so be forgiven, even by myself, or could I be better or worse than I am and still be the same, or is what's in my mind any different to what's on the screen black on white, and should I edit. And prune. And emend.

The bit of me that thinks I have no chance of survival outwith the trappings of civilisation knows that even this is as much true and as much false as I want it to be.

Must everything be known, and to whom? Even my deepest inadequacies?

I stood in his bathroom, for no reason other than that I was round his house because he was helping me out by doing a piece of work for me that I couldn't then do myself. The first time I saw him I was sitting at a desk in a large open room where maybe a dozen or so other people sat at or by desks, and we were all working on a project that was very exciting. It was exciting not because it had any meaning, but because the task was formidable, the challenge demanding, the technology thrilling; and the people assembled were good: they had crest-of-the-wave, or, as one of them liked to put it, 'bleeding edge' competencies. (I'm not sure I like the word 'competencies', but still; that's the kind of context we are talking about...) There was no more of a point to any of it than there ever was to any of these corporate projects, beyond making a big brand look like what its executives could be coaxed into thinking was 'cool', and apart from one product that this particular project now helped this particular brand launch that was pretty crap on the inside but won hands down on design, the world would not have been any worse a place without any of what we were doing being done, but as I was sitting at my desk, making up inane scenarios of attractive young people using handsets, in walked the most attractive young person I thought I had ever seen. (If you imagine this as a film, here is where the music swells and—depending on genre and era—we may just go into slow motion.)

Since then, and several years of sporadically working together later, we had settled into a comfortable arrangement whereby I adored him and he let me do so. I once drunkenly at a party told him that I would never do anything to jeopardise our friendship, and he, similarly drunkenly, had shrugged his shoulders and said something along the lines of 'that's good to know,' I can't quite remember. Whenever we went out as a group, which we did now and then before he got married, I completely failed to disguise my being smitten, which, after a while, became something of a running gag in said group: I adored him, he let me. There was nothing more to it. Now I'd asked him for a favour and he'd graciously said yes. I went round his house to help him do the work he was helping me out with and I went to the bathroom and there hung two of his shirts.

Maybe not everything needs to be told. Maybe some things are best left unsaid. Imaginations run wild. I stood close to his shirts that hung from a hook or a line on two hangers and guided one to my face and inhaled. Or did I think I would like to but just didn't dare? It was as if he were in the room: for a moment I felt, this is you. Two seconds, three seconds, four seconds, five. That's enough. You don't cling on to that which undoes you. Or maybe you do, in your mind.

This is and remains my unending flaw (I want to say 'tragic' but 'farcical' would be more accurate here): the realities of my heart are unhinged. I meet somebody, I fall for them, I imagine the world adjusted and changed, and I project onto them my idea of perfection and see a settled ideal that requires no more explanation. The other person, more likely than not, is oblivious to any of this, and if I make the mistake to draw their attention to it, they annihilate me with bewildered indifference, not unkind but bemused, not intentional, but lethal.

George has been looking at me as if he were studying me, and I wonder does he know who I am. Not 'know' as in possess factual evidence, of which none can exist, but know as in sense, as in experience that profound certainty—inaccurate though it be—that you have when you are in a reality that compels.

Ahmed arrives with our second mojito, and I think there would be something tremendously entertaining about getting drunk with myself. That would undoubtedly loosen things up, I fancy, if we both simply got plastered. Then again, it's still only about two, two thirty in the afternoon, I still don't know why I'm here at the Limonlu Bahçe in Istanbul, and I can't begin to think where I'll be spending the night, but then there is really no hurry about any of this, and it occurs to me: we could go for a walk. But that would entail leaving this delightful oasis, it would mean dodging traffic and weaving through throngs of people, and it would mean being reminded that there is a world out there that is simply there and cannot, in essence, be argued with; whereas here, in the speckled shade of the trees, and with Ahmed and his angular colleague our waiters, and with the mojitos softening the focus of perception, and with George in clearly no more of a hurry than I am, I feel safe and, more than comfortable, content. Content just to be, and to be here, for a little while longer.

I look at him and think: you're going to be just fine. Just don't make all the mistakes I've made and keep making, right to this day. I can be so very inept, sometimes.

He looks back at me, and I think he knows what I mean. And I say: 'I do not understand my heart at all.' And I don't.

{Seasons}

twinklings to
meanderings
fountains into streams:
we shimmer
then we die
though these be energies that linger

my early autumn, your late spring
our seasons out of synch, we could
if we were so inclined
nudge each a little, cheat
ourselves into a
summer
of untold delights –

say we were otherwise
compatible, we'd make
each other
perfect

11 The Wood Pixie

We called her The Wood Pixie. None of us knew her. Still, it pleased us to make mild fun of her, not in an evil, vicious, or ill-tempered way, more in an abstract helplessness: there was this woman who had the man we all loved, and he was beholden to her.

We imagined her as sharp and fierce and incredibly demanding. There is no telling whether we were right to do so; it was just an impression we got. Not only did we not know her, we also didn't ever really hear anything about her, other than that she existed. And so The Wood Pixie acquired mythical status, and whenever we found that he couldn't make it to a party or said no to a dinner or did not invite us to his wedding, we relished imagining her stamping angry little feet on the ground, conjuring demons and casting terrible spells.

Once in a while though, he managed to escape. He knew it would not be forever—we knew he wouldn't want it to be forever, because we knew, we imagined, he was already too lost to her—but just for an evening, now and then, or even, as on one occasion, for a weekend in the country, somewhere nobody would find us, he might be able to get away and join us.

Another of our good friends had borrowed a house. It was a very large house, a converted barn, with dark wooden beams, an incredibly high ceiling, deep leather sofas, and the kind of beds where you dream you have gone to heaven, even before you've fallen asleep.

We were there for only one night, I believe, and really absolutely nothing much happened: we arrived. We must at some point have eaten some food, we drank wine or more likely champagne, because that's what we tended to drink in those days, and we did a few lines. Maybe we played some games. Where the food or the wine or champagne or the lines had come from, I don't remember: they simply materialised. Much like the house.

Even precisely who was there now is a blur. Four of us, maybe six? Certainly no large group and certainly nobody we didn't know. I only remember him though, really, and obviously our host. I wished, I so longed, I hoped, I so willed the evening to get to the point where he would simply not care enough about who or what he normally was and forget about The Wood Pixie and allow me to snuggle up to him in his bed, and very possibly he would have done had I had the courage to sneak into it in the first place. But I didn't. *Non, je ne regrette rien, sauf... Sauf les temps quand je suis été lâche. Sauf les temps quand un amour ou une 'trame du hazard' semblait possible, mais je n'avais pas le courage de tenter ma chance.*

There have been two, maybe three, possibly, at a stretch, four. Two, three or four times when I didn't have the courage to take the chance that was obviously there. (Or was it only ever there in my—wishful—imagination?) The weakness of being vulnerable. The weakness of not being able to show yourself vulnerable. The need, at all cost, not to be needy.

Morning came and I woke up in a bedscape of white softness, on my own. It so happened that he gave me a lift home in his red MX5. And then the killer line, as we sat next to each other, in worn leather seats, shades on, burning down the M4:

I: 'That was a really excellent weekend.'

He: 'Yes, and the best thing about it is *getting away with it.*'

I saw The Wood Pixie looming suddenly large, puffed up to overbearing proportions, but even she, with her frightening powers of penetration, would never know about this weekend, because he'd make it home before her, all obedient innocence. And he was pleased as punch about this, beaming like a boy, his eyes on the fast lane, the one that would get him back just in time, under the radar.

Later on I then once or twice saw a picture of her: she looked lovely. There is no reason at all to assume—to presume—that he ended up with the wrong woman, the wrong person. In fact I imagine the opposite. For him, all things considered (if not quite all told), The Wood Pixie was probably pretty much perfect; and to this day, she most likely is just what he needs...

{Displacement}

As I sit watching George sip his mojito, slowly, deliberately, the memories of the past and the memories of the future congeal to form a slush into which my brain slowly dissolves. I feel it already trickling out of my ear. The right one, as my head is somewhat rightward inclined.

I was, I was beautiful. I never once thought so then, and I most certainly don't think me so now, but looking at myself then I cannot escape this devastating realisation: I was really beautiful.

My best friend in London, Michael, once asked, when looking at a picture of me from my teens, 'how did this'—he points at the picture—'turn into this': he gestures at me. Between me and George lie three decades of the unknown.

Must it, though, must it be so unknown. If I'd known then what I know now would I not have avoided so many mistakes? Would these regrets, three or four only, maybe, but two or three of them profound, not simply have turned into gorgeous memories of ever fulfilling wistfully relivable ecstasy? Unaided?

Soon, I want to say to my young self, you'll meet, quite by chance, a boy who is so roundly adorable, so sunny, so sweet, so entirely lovely, that you'll feel in a trance for six days around him. He will call you, on your answerphone, and say: 'Hello, it's Stefan here, I'm a friend of Soandso who's a friend of Beatrice. She said I could give you a call and maybe stay with you for a few days in London?' Once you live in London,

George, you will have friends and friends of friends, and of course family and friends of family come to visit: you will not want for guests!

On this particular occasion though you may not be so keen, you may only just have arrived in your first flatshare and not know the others too well, but in particular also your best friend from school, Peggy, may be staying with you, for six weeks as it happens. How you ever got that past your still new flatmates whom you don't really know yet will be beyond you once you get to the stage where you are me. But be that as it may, you will think—and Peggy will agree—and you both will be pretty much of a mind, that the last thing you need, or even want for that matter, is some strange boy who happens to be the friend of really in all seriousness an ex-girlfriend of yours to come and spoil your quality time together for you. You've never been one to say no, though, so you say yes, but you don't want to change your plans, and your plans for the night he arrives are to go to the theatre with Peggy, and so you say to him, just ring the buzzer, there'll be somebody around to let you in while we're out; you can sleep on the sofa, make yourself at home.

So you go out with your best friend from your school days, Peggy, and you have a lovely time, and then you get back home, and on the sofa there is this unbearably cute little face, tucked into a sleeping bag, happy as peaches in lala-land, and you know you're already a little in love. And you both look at him in unabashed wonder and you decide to let him sleep and when you all wake up in the morning you all feel like you've always been friends, and from then on you do practically everything together, you go out together, you drink together, you dance together; and at one point, and you don't quite know how, probably because Peggy happens to be at school, she is, after all, here to learn English, you find yourselves sitting next to each other on your slim single bed and he's wearing his funky skintight jeans and no top and you are wearing whatever it is you are wearing at the time, probably black, and you will nearly but not quite put your hand on his thigh or his hand and you bask in his presence and you cannot get over how beautiful is his torso, and how charming his smile and how big his blond hair, and you don't know how you do it but somehow you let the moment pass and nothing happens at all and you won't ever quite understand how you let that happen, because soon after he leaves and you write to each other once or twice only and he says something along the lines of he liked you and how wonderful a time you had together and that maybe it was better that nothing happened that day, it would only have spoilt things. This you will never be quite able to believe, you will forever know, deep at heart, that kissing him, holding him, caressing him, touching him, being with him would not have spoilt anything, it would simply have made those six days complete.

There'll be that, I want to tell my young self: don't let it happen like that, don't let that moment pass. Live it, grab it, make a fool of yourself, risk him saying you're overstepping a mark. It may be embarrassing, it may feel painful and cruel if he rejects you, but so is this, so is knowing you didn't seize that day, that half day even, so is knowing you lived one afternoon less than you could have, as it turns out should have done. One afternoon? An early lifetime. Precious,

precious days, while you are young. I want to extend my arm and put my tan and since late slightly freckled hand upon George's. When do you stop thinking 'what will he think?' At what point will you simply not care? But then, should you not care? Is not the other person as far away from you as you are from them? Could not they make the first move, or say the first word; be first to break the glass that divides you?

And then it hits you, out of the blue: they don't see the glass! They send all the signals, they make all the moves, they simply wonder why you don't respond, and you wonder how can they not know that you're surrounded by a bell made of glass: the sounds are muffled, the scent is dead, the gestures distorted, the temperature inside is always too high. The effort it takes you to break through to them is gargantuan. They just smile and think it strange that you barely smile back; the way that you read them would to them be entirely unintelligible. Suddenly it strikes you: you're under a bell, George, and you don't even know it.

I reach out to myself, but not to my hand, I put my hand on my shoulder instead. That seems to be more in tune with the overall situation. Oddly, this doesn't surprise young me. George looks back at me, half-knowing, half expectant; a look that, as a youth, you might give your grandparent who's about to say something really obvious, like: you're an intelligent boy.

Being thus indavertently cast in the role of my dad's father or my mum's mother startles me and I withdraw my hand, almost too quickly. I need to think of a reason for having put it on my shoulder in the first place and so I say: 'If you ever come to London, you must get in touch.' It sounds like a disingenuous offer, saying this to my younger self, but with anyone else in a comparable case it would be perfectly genuine, and pure of intent, too.

He nods gravely. It hasn't quite done the trick, I'm convinced, but George here seems to be un-further-perturbed. 'This is nice,' he says, in the involuntary generic understatement of the youth who hasn't yet mastered the language, about his mojito. It's oddly appropriate. This is nice, I agree without saying it, and instead I ask him if he wants another. Knowing now who I'm with, it doesn't surprise me that he says 'sure?' with an upward inflexion that suggests question where there ought to be assertion. The young. If only I could make it lighter for you, thinner, the bell, more penetrable, the fortress of isolation around you. You will find a way. You will find a way: I have found a way, so will you.

Advice time. I'm about to say something along the lines of: just do what you want to do your way, or, it's not going to be so easy, you know, but you'll somehow muddle through, or, deep in your heart you know that no matter what the ups and the downs, you're on a fairly stable track, like a roller coaster. And then it strikes me how ludicrous that is.

You're not on a track at all, you're in free flow. You have no way of knowing what's right or wrong for you, you have to find out step by perilous step. Sometimes it will feel ridiculously easy and other times it will feel impossible. They will not understand you. Seriously. They will smile, but they will think: what the fuck? You have the right to be whoever, whatever you want to be, everybody else has the right to think what the fuck. At times you will feel: nobody gets me. At all. You will be so alone in the world that you will want to sit in a corner and cry, and you will sit in the corner and cry. You will need to be stronger than you ever thought you could be, because sometimes they will not just think what the fuck, they will hate you and say so. And you will wonder what have I ever done to you that you hate me, I have written some words. I have thought some thoughts. I have put them out there. Ah, I have trodden on your reality by putting them out there. And then you have to say to yourself: I have the right to write words and think thoughts and to put them out there, they have the right to hate me for it. It is not wise nor generous, nor really humane, but sadly it's only human of them if they do so. Forgive them for being human.

Angular waitress is still nowhere to be seen, so once again I hold my hand up to Ahmed who takes my order for two more mojitos. 'These are nice,' I say to Ahmed, unnecessarily, 'could we have two more, please.' I wonder should I ask him at the same time if he knows a good place for me to stay, like a hotel he can recommend somewhere nearby, but then I realise what this might sound like to him, so instead I wait until Ahmed has gone, and I ask George here where he is staying. 'Round the corner, at a hostel.' To my utter relief George doesn't ask me where I'm staying: I just realise what a potential trap I've set myself, when it occurs to me that I have a discontinuity here. At the time when I'm George, this place most likely doesn't exist. It's too now. So, past me is in my world, not I in the world of past me. But my world at this point ought to be Kingston-upon-fucking-Thames. Practical considerations and logic have both been rendered imponderable, by what I know not.

What do you want to be when you grow up? I ask myself and I notice I'm not saying this out loud and so I can't tell whether this is Now Me asking Young Me or Young Me asking Now Me or Now Me asking Now Me or Young Me asking Young Me or all of Me at the same time.

Sundown. I shall wait until sundown. I shall hold out as long as George here holds out. I will I will just stay with me until sundown.

12 Tales From an Alternative Universe

At Nice airport I give a young man the eye, because he looks just like Peter, whom I know from a short shoot a while back and who happened to be in Cannes with his girlfriend about two years ago.

In a multiverse of all possible universes there is one in which I go up to him and say: 'Hello Peter, how are you?'

He doesn't know me, but by coincidence his name is actually Peter (he has that Peter glint in his eye), and he too thinks there's something familiar about me, something he recognises, and so, so as not to seem rude, he gamely says: 'hey, I'm very well, thanks, and you? – Are you here for the festival?' I say, 'yes.'

'Well, do you want a lift into Cannes, I'm here with my girlfriend?'

Ah, girlfriend here too, I think, but, why not? and I gladly accept. As we talk on the ride while his girlfriend is conversing in fluent French with the driver, we get along swimmingly, and by the time we reach Cannes, we sort of realise that we don't really know each other, but we both of us don't mind and if anything feel we should get to know each other better, and we both pretend to of course already have each other's numbers but let's exchange them anyway, just in case; and we hook up for dinner and then have drinks and arrange to meet up again the following night.

As it happens, his girlfriend is going to some do or other with some of her friends, so we'll probably just be the two of us, and after another dinner, a few more drinks and then just one or two more, we realise that we do have a lot more in common than one might at fist glance imagine, and even what we don't have in common we complement each other on perfectly, and so we probably have a bit of a kiss, maybe a cuddle. Perhaps even a bit of a snog. But then he thinks of his girlfriend and that he's supposed to be straight, which doesn't bother me too much (it happens to the best of people), but we go to see a couple of screenings the day after, and then his girlfriend and a few friends have invitations to a really quite excellent party on Monday, and we're tagging along there as well.

At some point we conspire to lose them, or they us, and we suddenly find ourselves alone again and peacefully zonked, on the beach, with the still mild air drifting in softly, and us drifting off equally softly, together, and by Tuesday, my last day, I wake up next to him, and he's actually there, and I realise: no, this wasn't a dream and the wedding will probably be some time next summer...

I'm reminded of the incident with the handbag. The incident with the handbag happened with a man I could have imagined marrying, could perhaps still imagine, if not marrying then being together with, easily, comfortably, steadily. Uncomplicated. It happened before he married someone else.

We were out drinking, as on occasion we would, and after doing so to quite some extent we took a cab home, as on occasion we did. We got into my bed to curl up with each other, as on occasion we might, to literally just sleep with each other, when he reached down his side of the bed and lifted up a nondescript brown leather bag and said: 'and here's the handbag.'

That made no more sense to me then than it does now, but I was categorically drunk, and so was he, and I had my arm around him and I could not expect of myself—nor was I able to think that the world could expect of me—to compute the significance of such a statement and gesture at this particular juncture. He dropped the bag back down on the floor and leant into my chest and fell asleep, as did I, almost immediately.

In the hungover morning I held on to him for as long as I could, which was never quite long enough, but he had to go to work, and I said I would deal with the bag. The bag, it turned out, was an ordinary woman's handbag with the ordinary things you'd find in a bag: not that I looked through the bag in any detail, that would have felt intrusive. I fished out the mobile and called the number labelled 'mum'. I told a bemused lady that by circumstances which I couldn't strictly explain but that involved a friend and too much alcohol, I found myself, somewhat involuntarily, in custody of, most likely, her daughter's handbag, and was keen to restore it to her forthwith. There must have been a follow-up conversation with the daughter herself (presumably on her home phone?) and it transpired that the daughter in question was an actress currently performing at a West End theatre, and that she had been out with a friend after the show and ended up for a drink at the same bar as we did. She was gracious if a little taken aback, but then who can blame her. We arranged that I would bring her her bag to the stage door. I picked up a bunch of flowers and a bottle of wine and brought her the bag, apologising profusely on behalf of my friend. My friend never mentioned the matter again. Nor did I. The actress may well have thought that my friend was imaginary and that I just hadn't been brave enough to come clean entirely, but what did it matter.

Which is perhaps why I am reminded of this incident in the first place: it just didn't matter. And I thought: this is what it would be like, would it not, to have a partner, an 'other half,' when they did something inexplicable, and it really just didn't matter. I know him well enough to know he wasn't stealing a woman's handbag. There was never any chance of him, or me, taking anything out of it and keeping it. And it obviously fell to me to return the bag to its owner, because I was capable of doing so and I had the time to do so, while he had a job to go to, in Pentonville prison of all places. Plus I had sufficient distance from the incident itself to just handle it factually. It made no sense at all, but it made perfect sense. And so to this day I don't know why it even happened. But then what do we ever know?

(I once spent about an hour or so, incidentally, on the phone to someone who didn't know me, nor I him. I'd recently arrived in London, I was living in my first flatshare in Gloucester Terrace and we had a plastic payphone in the hall. It rang. I answered. He said, hello can I speak to George, I said, this is George speaking, and we talked. About all manner of things. For quite a while. A long while. I had no idea who he was, but he sounded nice and I was new to town so I assumed that sooner or later the universe would reveal to me whom I was having a conversation with, probably somebody I recently met and hadn't quite filed anywhere in my brain yet. Then he asked me how my new job was going and I said, what new job? I'd been in my job for six months now, it was my first permanent job since I moved here. And then we realised we didn't actually know each other. We laughed and told each other it was nice talking and wished each other a good life and hung up. I wonder does he still tell the story as I do?)

What do we ever really know...

{Afterthought}

Every so often—ever so rarely—that feeling of a cold clean blade sliding under my skin and lifting the tissue off my bones: I can't help but stare; not stare, but gaze upon in wonder.

I pretend to play *Jass* on my phone;
I do play *Jass* on my phone, but my concentration is shot, I don't remember what's gone; I can see what is trump but I no longer care what it means: the boy sitting opposite on the tube, he's not a boy, he's a man; in his salmon coloured trousers with his caramel shoes over deep navy socks; his deep sea green jumper (or is that navy too?) his light glacier lake coloured shorts, showing a bit only between shirt and belt, a soft plain material, not briefs and not boxers; his finesculpted lips, his

long dark chestnut hair and the ever-a-tad-absent expression. His tallness. The strength of his thighs by comparison.

He alights at Victoria.

I pull myself together. I have to pull myself together. I've written a book about him. About him and about all the others: there are only two or three or three or four, they are so so rare and so precious and so, so incomprehensibly beautiful. Let not it be said that I did not draw from that beauty the vernating breath of a melancholy yen.

Oh to be nineteen and a poet. Was I ever nineteen? I was once a poet; albeit briefly. Perhaps I can be so again...

www.ingramcontent.com/pod-product-compliance
Ingram Content Group UK Ltd.
Pitfield, Milton Keynes, MK11 3LW, UK
UKHW041842200726
13854UKWH00005BA/198

9 781643 704517